azores

island to island

açoresnatural

PUBLISHED BY
Ver Açor, lda.

EDITORIAL COORDENATION
Ver Açor, Lda.

PHOTOGRAPHY BY
Ver Açor, Lda. ©
Fernando Resendes
José António Rodrígues
Nuno Sá

TEXT BY
José Damião Rodrigues
Ricardo Madruga da Costa

TRANSLATION
Marília Pavão

GRAPHIC DESIGN BY
Selecor-Artes Gráficas
Helder Segadães

FINAL ARTWORK BY
Selecor-Artes Gráficas

PRE-PRINTING AND PRITING BY
Selecor-Artes Gráficas

LEGAL DEPOSIT
Nº 261195/07

ISBN
989-95141-9-5

Porto, 2007

Copyright © 2007
Ver Açor, Lda.
All rights reserved
Published by Ver Açor, Lda.
Rua dos Afonsos, 8
9500-377 Ponta Delgada - Açores
Telf./Fax 296 684 926 - Mobile phone 917 377 310
veracor@veracor.pt
www.veracor.pt

açoresnatural

azores

island to island

To Jackson and Rico,
   Enjoy your sailing in these beautiful islands. Good luck and safe sailing.

   With love from,

   Patricia and Chris.

veaçor | editores ©

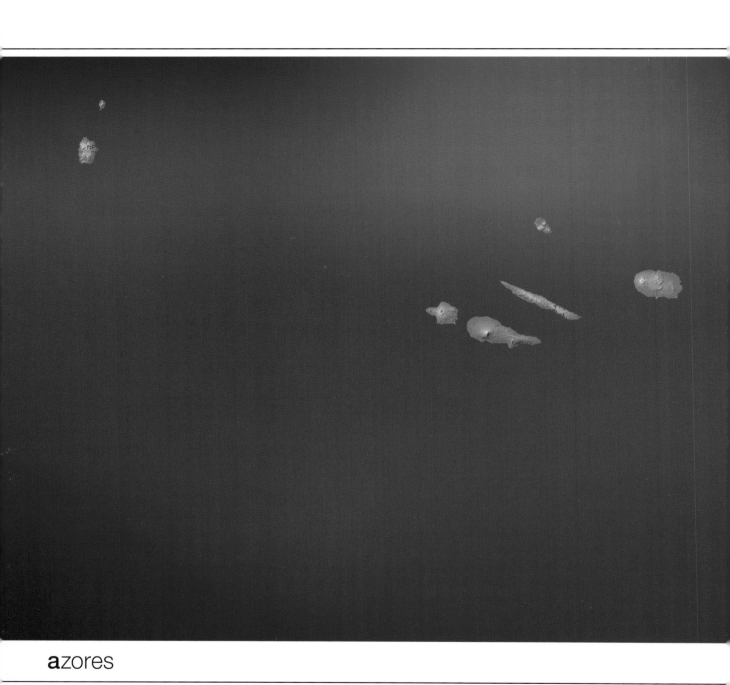

azores

table of contents

azores

Located at the heart of the Northern Atlantic, the first islands of the Azores were discovered in 1427, and today, we know them as the eastern and central groups of the archipelago. In a later exploration further west, possibly around 1452, the navigators found the islands of Flores and Corvo, which constitute the western group. Anchored in the middle of the ocean as if they were basaltic ships, the Azorean islands have been poetically described by the great Azorean writer Vitorino Nemésio as "volcanic clusters underneath clouds that are wings and animals that are clouds". In this way, the writer brings forward the geological matrix of these islands and relates it to the islanders' feelings that balance between the love of the land and the love of adventure that pulls them to the sea, in the eagerness of the journey to be.

The islands' volcanic nature has manifested itself throughout the centuries, disturbing the islanders' daily life. Amongst the most relevant eruptions, the highlights go to the island of Pico (1562-1564), Fogo's Lake (São Miguel, 1563-1564), Furnas (São Miguel, 1630), the island of Faial (1672-1673), Pico (1718 and 1720) and to the island of São Jorge (1808). As for earthquakes, the most important manifestations were the ones that destroyed the first town of Vila Franca do Campo (São Miguel, 1522) and, recently, the one that shattered the city of Angra do Heroísmo (Terceira), on the first day of 1980.

The daily experience of these events, along with the attacks by pirates that frequently occurred in the islands of Santa Maria, Graciosa, São Jorge, Flores and Corvo, have had a strong influence on the profound religious traditions of the Azoreans. Moreover, the awareness of their isolation as islanders, which heightens solidarity amongst the islands' inhabitants, has also shaped the way in which these people live their faith. An unmistakable display of this religiousness happens during the festivities dedicated to the Holy Spirit when people offer food and drink to whomever passes by in a thanksgiving celebration.

For many centuries, and in addition to the frail living conditions, the Azoreans lived under a social model

São Miguel, Furnas

Flores, lakes

Espirito Santo's festivities,
crown

Igreja da Misericórdia,
Angra-church

Grape harvest, Pico

that intensified the differences between the privileged and the non-privileged, thus reinforcing the need for change which came in the form of emigration. The first emigrants left the archipelago in the 16th century, and the fleeing from the islands increased in the following centuries, especially to Brazil (18th and 19th centuries) and to North America (20th century).

In the course of its history, the Azores have actively participated in the life of the Atlantic and have been the stage for many historical battles that marked the competition between rival powers over the ruling of the oceans and of several overseas' territories. Although distant from the American and European shores, the islands, particularly the richest, more central ones, were not left stranded from the political scene of the kingdom and of the world. Due to its strategical location on the sea route system, and after the Iberian Union that reunited Portugal with the Kingdom of Castile, the Castilian troops settled in Angra do Heroísmo from 1583 to 1642. Meanwhile, in the heat of the battle over the domination of the Atlantic and the world, the English often attacked the islands in the attempt to build a naval base. Throughout the 17th and 18th centuries, the ones that tormented the islanders were the Magrebian pirates who usually captured some of the inhabitants and took them as slaves. In more recent centuries, and still in the arena of international power, the Azores have been under the sight of several of the world's powers. Whether as a stage for naval battles or through the setting up of military bases, the Azores have continuously demonstrated their strategic relevance for the world's power balance.

Nevertheless, the importance of the archipelago, to Portugal and to the world, is not confined to this sole dimension. The Azores also bear a great importance in what concerns the economic field. The islands' original flora was mainly characterised by trees like cedar, dogwood, "pau-branco", beech, laurel, yew, and by heath. The former were mostly cut down to give place to farming land, thus opening the way for the archipelago to become Portugal's main wheat supplier. Since the end of the 15th century, and due to São Miguel and Terceira's large production, the archipelago supplied not only mainland Portugal, but also Madeira, the Moroccan military strongholds, and the naval fleet. By the middle of the 16th century, following a plague that destroyed the grain fields, the islands' producers redirected their production towards dyeing plants, namely dyer's woad which was eagerly sought by the European fabric manufacturers. However, this production would slowly disappear throughout the 17th century. Although wheat production never quite disappeared from the islands, after the 18th century it was corn that took the stand, alongside the export of oranges from the island of São Miguel, which brought wealth to many families in the island. Meanwhile, in the central group islands, the role played by dyer's woad and oranges was performed by wine and by a local kind of brandy ("aguardente"). These were exported to the Americas from Horta's harbour which became the main commercial stop between the islands and the western Atlantic, especially in what refers to the British colonies, from the end of the 17th century onwards.

In the second half of the 19th century, and as an answer to the vine and orange crisis, the wit of the Azorean landlords and businessmen turned the islands' agriculture towards the production of pineapple, tea, tobacco and other industrial products like sugar beet. From the second half of the 20th century on, almost concurrently with the new political cycle started by 25th April 1974's revolution, the islands' economy has been rooted in animal husbandry and in dairy products. However, in the last few years, there has been an increased focus on the tourism industry, due to the archipelago's high touristic potential. On one hand, we have the renovation of urban buildings which promotes the value of museological and cultural spaces, such as Colégio dos Jesuítas (former church; today, a sacred art museum) or Teatro Micaelense (theatre), both situated in Ponta Delgada.

Faial, view from Pico

Tourists on a whale watching trip

On the other hand, we have the boost of eco-tourism, which harmoniously takes advantage of the islands' lavish vegetation and of the warm waters of the Gulf Stream that circle the archipelago. Footways and pathways, parks and natural reserves, UNESCO classified sites, and sea activities, such as diving, whale watching and big game fishing, are just some of the possibilities that Azorean nature offers its visitors, in a celebration of its unique qualities.

Marina, Faial

santa maria

The most southerly island of the Azores, Santa Maria, was the first island to be discovered in 1427. It was also the first to hear about the news that there was land far beyond the horizon, towards west, as Columbus stopped there on his way back from the Indies in 1493. Nevertheless, its location further south, in conjunction with its small size and relevance, did not bring benefits. For example, the pirates from Argel and from other nations took advantage of its isolation and attacked it frequently, pillaging and taking its inhabitants as slaves.

However, its geographical location has provided the island with a unique climate that highlights the excellence of its beaches - São Lourenço, Praia Formosa - , paradisiacal sites which bear the promise of transforming Santa Maria into a prime-choice tourist destination. Until then, there is the international music festival - *Maré de Agosto* - that takes place every August at Praia Formosa and which has been gaining importance in the World Music circuit, bringing musicians and music lovers from all over the world to the island of the sun.

Besides its climate and beaches, this island has other interesting particularities. Its small villages, like Santo Espírito, are as peculiar as the impressive landscape that marks places like Maia, with its natural amphitheatre layout filled with terraces that nestle the vineyards inside basaltic squares that can only be reached through narrow, steep stairways built in the rock. São Lourenço is another remarkable place. Its shell-like design has naturally developed the ideal location for the vineyards that colour the black rock with their green foliage, whilst its bay welcomes the crystal-clear waters of the Atlantic. This is just an example of what is offered to you by this little island, also known as the island of Gonçalo Velho (its first captain - donee).

São Lourenço's Bay

Traditionall windmill

Maia

Rural life

Traditional house

Praia Formosa

Barreiro da Faneca

Maia, lighthouse

São Lourenço, vineyards

Grape harvest

são miguel

Initially associated with Santa Maria, São Miguel started being recognised on its own from 1474 onwards. Considered to be "the islands' barn" and, later on, the relief supplier of the island of Madeira and of North Africa's military strongholds, São Miguel marked the economy of the Atlantic archipelagos. After wheat export, and on the turn of the 16th century, came the boom of dyer's woad production, which was followed by the orange cycle that brought hundreds of ships to the island's harbour in search of the fruit. This was one of the wealthiest periods of São Miguel's society, bringing forth gentlemen farmers like Hickling, Burnett, Ivens, Read and Cockburn, alongside the more noble and traditional families such as Câmaras, Botelhos, Arrudas, Andrades, amongst many others.

Due to its dimensions and population (over 50% of the archipelago's total), which allowed for its increasing wealth and provided for the development of its industries, São Miguel has become the richest and most developed island in the archipelago. Moreover, it also displays an enormous variety of astonishing landscapes that make of it one of the jewels of this garden that is the Azores. Sete Cidades and Vista do Rei, Fogo and Furnas' Lakes, "wonder of the Azorean volcanism" (Vitorino Nemésio), are just some of the names that travel the world, advertising that in the middle of the Atlantic there is a place where nature's exoticism and exuberance have found their dwelling.

Amongst local productions, the ex-libris is pineapple, which was introduced in the island by the end of the 19th century. This fruit is grown inside greenhouses that are mostly located in the outskirts of the city of Ponta Delgada, and that are definitely worth a visit. Another highlight goes to tea whose plantations are located on the northern coast of the island (Gorreana and Porto Formoso). It is possible to visit both factories and witness the production and processing stages.

The wealth and prestige of the local landlords can still be seen in the beautiful manor houses and orchards that are spread around the island, such as Solar de Nossa Senhora das Necessidades in Livramento (17th century), or Solar de Nossa Senhora do Vencimento, located in the western part of the city of Ribeira Grande, and whose chapel is mentioned already in

Povoação, partial view

Sete Cidades, lakes

Ponta Delgada

Pottery

Caloura

Santa Bárbara's beach

Southern coast

1670. To these manor houses, we can add beautiful botanical gardens like Jardim António Borges (Ponta Delgada) and Terra Nostra Park (Furnas) with specimens from all over the world. In what refers to religious architecture, we can draw attention, in the city of Ponta Delgada, to the Manueline-style portal of the Mother-Church, to São Pedro's church, and to the baroque façade of Colégio dos Jesuítas' church, which dates back to the 18th century. In Vila Franca do Campo, the highlights go to the Mother-Church while, in Lagoa, they go to the Franciscan monastery, which dates back to the 17th century.

In what pertains to erudite culture, the island's symbols are Antero de Quental (1842-1891), poet and philosopher, and Teófilo Braga (1843-1924), who was Portugal's President in 1915. Along with these

Lagoa do Fogo, Lake

fundamental intellectual figures, there is also the autonomic movement of the 19th century, which left an unquestionable legacy to the architects of the archipelago's new political era. There are also the outstanding collections of literary works that can be seen in Biblioteca Pública e Arquivo Regional de Ponta Delgada (Ponta Delgada's Public Library and Regional Archive), amongst which can be found the original of *Saudades da Terra*, by Gaspar Frutuoso (1522-1591, friar and historian), and the compilations of the Canto's

brothers (Ernesto, Jose e Eugénio). In the field of art, we can draw attention to the works of Canto da Maya (1890-1981, sculptor), and of Domingos Rebelo (1891-1975, painter), whose works can be seen at Museu Carlos Machado, housed in a former convent of Clarisse nuns (1567).

The ancestral religiousness of the Azorean people has one of its main demonstrations in the pilgrim groups of men that travel around the island during Lent. These are known as *romeiros* and they walk around the

Pineapple plantation

Sete Cidades

Gorreana, tea plantation

Traditional fishing boats

Southern coast

Igreja Matriz
de Nª Srª da Estrela,
Ribeira Grande
Mother - church

Folk dance

Cavalhadas de São Pedro,
Ribeira Grande
Maia   (Festivities to honour Saint Peter)

Sete Cidades

Salto do Cavalo, panoramic belvedere

Caldeira Velha, Ribeira Grande

Ponta Delgada, panoramic view

island for eight days, visiting the chapels and churches dedicated to the Virgin Mary. Another massive religious manifestation occurs during the festivities dedicated to Senhor Santo Cristo dos Milagres. These festivities occur in Ponta Delgada and are related to the worship of the statue that goes by that name, which can be visited at Nossa Senhora da Esperança's convent (1541).

Today, on the island's southern coast, in the place were, in the beginning, there was "a solitary, god-forsaken, miserable place" and afterwards, "a small town" (Gaspar Frutuoso), we can find the most dynamic and entrepreneurial city of the Azores, bubbling with life and progress. Ponta Delgada brings together its ancestral values with the ongoing process of progressing. With *Portas do Mar*, a project designed to develop the city's waterfront, with the implementation of a cruise ship dock and passenger terminal and the development of the local marine leisure market, Ponta Delgada will definitely embrace the sea that nourishes it. Modernity intertwined by a renewed intimacy with the surrounding sea will not only enrich the city, but also the island's tourist infrastructures.

Sete Cidades (detail)

Furnas, Lake

Furnas, thermal springs

Furnas, Fumaroles

Romeiro (pilgrim)

Senhor Santo Cristo's
procession, Ponta Delgada

Romeiros (pilgrims)

Vila Franca's Islet

Sete Cidades, sunrise

Nordeste, natural park

Bruges, Corte-Reais, Cantos da Provedoria das Armadas, Ornelas, amongst many other illustrious families have played an important role in the history of this island, the third (terceira) to be discovered. As Gaspar Frutuoso claimed, Angra was "the universally renowned port of call of the west" when, during the 16th century, the Cape Route included it in the spice trade from India. During this wealthy period of Portugal's history, Angra became the most thriving city in the Azores, and throughout the centuries, it has maintained its essential importance in the development of the archipelago. It became the diocese's base in 1534, it housed the powerful Castilian troops from 1583 to 1642, and it was the general-captaincy of the archipelago from 1766 to 1832. Therefore, it is only natural that churches and palaces sprung up from every corner of its streets, transforming it into one of the most elegant cities in the world, as UNESCO recognised by awarding it the title of World Heritage City.

The justification for such an award can be witnessed through the preservation of the traditional urban architecture of downtown Angra, where simple houses stand alongside beautiful palaces, such as Palácio Bettencourt (the city's public library and regional archive), which displays an exquisite coat of arms on its façade, in manor houses like Solar de Nossa Senhora dos Remédios, Cantos Provedores das Armadas, Mãe de Deus, or in some of the houses in São Pedro. In the other city of Terceira, Praia da Vitória, named after the liberals' victory in 1829, the highlights go to its remarkable Mother-Church and to its Gothic-Manueline portal, whilst rural architecture has its essential representation in the village of Ramo Grande. Also worthy a visit is the former town of São Sebastião whose Mother-Church also possesses a noteworthy Manueline-style portal.

Angra has always played a fundamental role in the somewhat troublesome history of Portugal. It welcomed the resistance movement against the Spanish occupation from 1581 to 1583, and it helped to keep alive the freedom flame of the fights of 1820. These are just some of the historical episodes that can be revisited at Museu de Angra do Heroísmo

Urban architecture, Angra do Heroísmo

Ribeirinha

Igreja Matriz de Angra, Mother-church

Império da Caridade

Igreja da Misericórdia,
Angra do Heroísmo,
church

(museum), housed in the Baroque building of the former Convento de São Francisco (convent). In the same way they cherish their history, the people of Terceira are strongly attached to their traditional values and customs, both religious and profane. This can be witnessed through cultural manifestations such as *danças de espada* (sword dance) and *bailinhos* so dear to the Carnival's tradition, grievous melodies that talk about saudade, or sarcastic, yet amusing, musical duels that happen between two singers of improvisations (*cantigas ao desafio*). During summertime, there are daily *touradas à corda* (street bullruns) that draw enthusiastic crowds all around the island. In a culmination of this tribute to life and joy, there are the festivities to honour the Holy Ghost, when passers by are offered sweet bread and milk in a thanksgiving celebration. To this enjoyment of life, we can add the island's wonderful gastronomy whose

main representative is *alcatra à moda da Terceira* (top-sirloin cooked with spices and wine in a clay pan), which should always be accompanied by *vinho de cheiro* (local wine variety).

Therefore, there is no strategic relevance, no diplomatic conundrum, nor military base (Lajes) that can prevent Terceira's people from enjoying life like no other island in the archipelago does.

Espírito Santo, coroação (procession to honour the Holy Spirit)

Espírito Santo, bodo (offerings of bread and milk to honour the Holy Spirit)

Traditional pastry

Cantadores
(traditional singers)

Rural life

Tourada à corda, street bullfight

São João's festivities

Cidade de Angra and Monte Brasil

Algar do Carvão

Cerrados

Pastures

Praia da Vitória

graciosa

Unsuspected and magnificent, it is in the bosom of this island that one of the well-kept secrets of the Azores is hidden: Furna do Enxofre. Built after nature's whim, a gigantic dome glitters in polychromatic shades when the sunlight hits its walls. The dome vanishes into the darkness by a small lake whose waves kiss the pebbles of the irregular floor whilst the pounding sound of a small caldera reminds us that the origins of such a place are lost in time. His Serene Highness, Albert I, Prince of Monaco, in a risky descent, suspended by a rope, did not resist to the beauty of this place, during his visit to the archipelago in the end of the 19th century.

Opposite scenery is the one you have the chance to enjoy, as we climb to the top of Monte da Ajuda. There, you can breathe in the serenity that exudes from the simplicity of a small town, and as your eyes wander over the plane in front of you, the chequerboard of basaltic rock corrals stands out with the green vine leaves contrasting with the centenary black rocks. Here is grown one of Graciosa's ex-libris: the vine, which has provided the support for so many families along the years. In one of the town's streets, you will find an ethnographic museum - Museu Etnográfico - where you can revisit the ways of living of the older generations. Here, the highlights go to viticulture with the display of antique wine presses, memories of a long-lost era.

Habitually mentioned because of his brief references to Graciosa in his *Mémoires d'Outre-Tombe*, Chateaubriand undeniably did not have the privilege of delighting his eyes with the gracefulness of this island, after which it was named: *Graciosa* (graceful).

Santa Cruz

Fishing harbour

Caldeira

Furna do Enxofre

Baleia's islet

Shucking corn

Farol da Ponta da Barca
(lighthouse)

Traditional windmill

são jorge

As you look over the green plane pastures from Miradouro das Brenhas (panoramic terrace), you may contemplate the most thriving heather in the Azorean plateaus. If to this we add the pleasure taken from the adventure of descending the pathway towards the most humble of the island's *fajãs* - Fajã dos Bodes - , you will have retained the most relevant features of the rural landscapes of São Jorge. Another of the island's best well-kept secrets is the small church of Santa Bárbara, in the village of Manadas. Originally built in 1485 and rebuilt in the 17th century, it has an exquisite interior covered in polychromatic wood carvings dating back to 1770. Then, you have the sea, always the sea, with its waves framing the *fajãs* (small areas of flat land by the sea caused by the collapse of cliffs), where laborious people built small villages, in a defying challenge to the storms and to the ocean.

Standing as the north-western "bank" of the channel that links "the islands of the triangle" (Pico, Faial and São Jorge), São Jorge conceals some of the most beautiful landscapes of these islands. Already in the beginning of the 19th century, explorers like the Bullar brothers enjoyed the pleasure of crossing the waters that connect São Jorge to the other islands, while pirates like René Duguay-Trouin, who attacked and pillaged the town of Velas in 1708, may have lingered in the island's beauty. A century later (1808), the threats to the population were of a different sort, as a violent volcanic eruption buried lives and possessions. This intimate link that connects the islanders to the telluric nature of these islands can be witnessed in the church bell tower that defiantly stands tall, surrounded by lava flows. At the sacred art museum, in the interior of the temples, and in other museological sites, you will be able to revisit the history of this almost enchanted island.

Also in São Jorge, the festivities to honour the Holy Ghost have a fundamental importance in the islanders' life. Tradition is highly respected, as proved in the production of its worldwide renowned cheese. Still in the gastronomy field, but in a sweeter area, *espécies* with their hint of spice are a must-have, whilst the wool bedspreads, woven by the women of Fajã dos Vimes, are one of the island's most cherished symbols. This is São Jorge, with its fair-skinned people with freckles that descend from one of the first settlers, the Flemish Van der Haggen.

Velas

Northern coast

Fajã dos Cubres

Pathway to Fajã do Santo Cristo

Topo

Rural life

Hydrangeas bordering a pathway

Cheese industry

Pico's mountain, view from São Jorge

Around the middle of the 19th century, Thomas Wentworth Higginson, intentional visitor to these islands and friend of the Dabney family, described Pico and its mountain in such terms that it will be hard to supplant him. Only a high poetical sensitivity boosted by the overwhelming beauty of that ever-changing, wondrous mountain could have compared the tenuous fumarole that can be sighted over its bluish top to a censer, as if Pico was the altar of its own gratitude.

Previously to Higginson, the mountain-island had already caused a lasting impression in other travellers. In July 1775, during their stay in Faial, Johann Reinhold Foster (father) and Georg Foster (son), naturalists that accompanied James Cook in his second world circum-navigation, were led to believe that due to the size of the volcano, Pico was the largest island in the archipelago. In reality, the largest island is São Miguel.

From the top of Pico's mountain, as you your eyes wander over the immense plane filled with perfectly square, basaltic rock corrals that nestle the vineyards, you will have the chance of contemplating the most astonishing and dramatic landscape men has ever built in the archipelago. If to this we add the nature-made, erratic *maroiços* (high, pyramidal basaltic rocks) that remind us of long-lost rituals, the wonder is complete. A testimony of the permanent struggle between men and nature is the extensive vineyard landscape that has been classified by UNESCO as World Heritage Cultural Landscape as it "reflects a unique response to viniculture on a small volcanic island and one that has been evolving since the arrival of the first settlers in the 15th century. The extraordinarily beautiful man-made landscape of small, stone walled fields is testimony to generations of small-scale farmers who, in a hostile environment, created a sustainable living and much-prized wine" (UNESCO, 2004). To smooth the roughness of this rocky setting, the island displays a green plateau where you can find heather, beech and orange-berry pittosporum trees, which seem to contemplate the distant silhouettes of Faial and São Jorge. Amid the wide-ranging shades of green that cover the island, it is impossible not to notice the "mistérios" (lava fields)

Grape harvest

that spread the black of the volcanic rock in "lajidos" (pahoehoe lava flows whose smooth surface resembles slabs), always reminding us that the ruler of these islands is mother-nature.

At Museu dos Baleeiros (Whalers' Museum) and Museu do Vinho (Wine Museum), the island shares with the visitor what has been its way of living for centuries. Men's daily toil is represented by their work tools which include the ones used in the festivities dedicated to the Holy Ghost whose protection the islanders still seek. As a thanksgiving celebration, they organise beautiful festivities that honour the deep solidarity that links the inhabitants of this breathtaking island to its divine creator.

Still in Pico, in the town of Madalena, we may find one of the most emblematic representations of the political imagery of the pre-industrial Azorean societies. In Madalena's Town Hall, above its front door, there is a coat of arms that displays two birds (goshawks that represent the Azores) flanking Portugal's royal coat of arms, thus portraying the unity between the central power and the islands.

Whaling boats

Whale Museum, Lajes

Lava flows

Ancoradouro, harbour   Traditional costumes

faial

As a journalist once said, Faial should always be reached by sea, in an evocation of past sea journeys in tall ships and steamers that gradually unveiled the island as they got closer, journeys that always ended with the sight of Monte da Guia and Monte da Espalamaca, two arms waiting to embrace the traveller. In this bay, nestled in the arch drawn by the coastline, there was the harmonious amphitheatre of the city - Horta - where one could sight the exotic domes that crowned the convents and monasteries that Carmelites, Franciscans and Jesuits built in this city. In the uneven alignment of the streets, there were simple houses whose welcoming whiteness concealed the rough urban modesty that disembarkation revealed to the newly arrived passengers.

In the slow plough of the ships' keel, in a lazy approach to the island, Faial unveiled itself and revealed the freshness of its multishaded greenery that crawled all the way up to the mysterious Caldeira with its gigantic crater hidden inside, in an enchanted testimony of the island's birth. This is how the first encounter with the island was, a mixture of discovery and excitement to those who anxiously waited to reach land, after days or weeks of uncomfortable rolling and frustrated looks at the horizon which kept on hiding land.

The hundreds of sailboats that annually stop at the magnificent Marina of Horta - North-Atlantic's Yachting Capital - renew the sortilege of such discovery and excitement. In return, they offer the spectacular and colourful display of their flags, which give Horta the festival feel that fills it during summertime. Right next to the Marina, there is Santa Cruz's Castle, a witness of Cumberland (1589) and Essex's (1597) pirate attacks that destroyed the town and terrified its inhabitants.

Once you are on the island, coming across the Flemish reminiscences takes you back to the 15th century. For instance, the city's name - Horta - was chosen after the first captain - donee's name, Josse van Hurtere. Along with the daring splendour of its baroque churches (e.g. mother - church), and in the middle of the humble houses, you will spot the old buildings of the submarine communication cable companies that chose Faial as a main point for the attachment of

Caldeira, Faial

transatlantic communication cables (beginning of the 20th century - 1950's).

With the simple, bucolic beauty of its landscape, Faial offers its visitors the refreshing greenery of its hills that lead to the depths of the Caldeira that conceals and preserves precious specimens of the endemic vegetation which can also be observed at the local Botanical Garden, located at Flamengos. Nevertheless, the island's major attraction is undoubtedly the Capelinhos' volcano site. Situated on the westernmost point of the island, Capelinhos' bare desolation is probably the most unusual and original landscape of this archipelago. Here, we become aware of these islands' original process of formation. Its scars are visible in the hard basaltic rock, reminding us all of the adventurous and painful paths that the Azoreans had, and still have, to cross, in order to live here.

Peter Café Sport

Marina, Horta

Horta and Monte da Guia

Horta's harbour

A fisherman at Horta's harbour

Porto Pim's Bay

Igreja Matriz da Horta,
Mother-church

Horta

Capelinhos, volcano

flores

Europe's last frontier, on the borderline of the "American Channel", Flores was a vigilant sentinel of the Eastern Indies' fleets and Castilian ships that crossed the Atlantic. Tennyson praised Flores' name in an evocative poem that celebrated the memorable naval battle that caused the death of Sir Richard Grenville, onboard the legendary *Revenge* (1591). Although this is a circumstantial mention, it stands as a symbol, as Flores is the island that most frequently and more closely experienced the pirate attacks and pillage that devastated the Atlantic islands. Pirates from Elizabeth's England, buccaneers from other unknown origins, "insurgents" from Buenos Aires who had as main figure Almeidinha, born in Rabo de Peixe (São Miguel), ships in flames wrecked in battles between Her British Majesty's fleet and buccaneer ships sponsored by the young American republic; devastating attacks on the Yankee whalers by the famous *Alabama* (confederate vessel), which brought dozens of castaways to the island... These are just some examples of the saga that has been to live on this island, a result of the crown's neglect.

Totally opposite of this is today's Flores. Nowadays, Flores is the most exuberant expression of the beauty that characterises the Azorean islands. There are not enough adjectives to describe the wondrous splendour of this island as we focus on the variety and diversity of delights that can be found in such a small space. A myriad of lakes spread amongst an endless sea of blue hydrangeas; deep valleys that reveal dreamlike sceneries; waterfalls that plunge into the sea in an inebriating display of freshness; streams that flow amid luxurious greens... This is Flores: the most beautiful jewel in the Azorean crown.

Lagoa das Patas

Fajã Grande, sunbathing area

Fajã Grande

Fajãzinha

Corvo on the horizon

Watermill

Lagoa Rasa

Rocha dos Bordões

Lages

corvo

It was only in 1548 that the definite settlement of Corvo occurred, by the initiative of Gonçalo de Sousa, its captain-donee. For centuries, its residents felt abandoned by their rulers, in such a way that in 1768, the 700 settlers of Corvo asked the king permission to leave the island, in search for wider lands.

Nevertheless, they stayed, and by a nature's whim, all the islands of the Azores fit into it, as they are represented by small patches of land that seem to float in the midst of the calm waters of Caldeirão (crater-lake), in a unique and precise portrait of the nine islands' shape and number. Surprising the visitor, the striking scenery of Caldeirão seems almost out of proportion when compared to Corvo's small dimensions. It is as if the island could not contain it. After visiting Caldeirão, you can wander through the streets of the most medieval town of the archipelago, untouched by modern days' aggression. This will enable you to imagine how it is to live in this quiet, idle isolation, even if there is a plane that regularly visits the island.

The pirates from Argel that ventured through these waters, shielded by this forgotten island, certainly did not fall for its beauty as what lured them was pillage, not awe.

Corvo

Flores, view from Corvo

Vila Nova do Corvo, street

Traditional windmills

Beach

Caldeirão

Vila Nova do Corvo

photos by   Ver Açor, Lda. ©

Fernando Resendes:
- pages: 8 (right), 10 (top), 16 (top), 17 (bottom), 18 (left), 20, 22, 24, 25 (bottom), 26 (top), 27, 28, 34 (bottom), 35 (right), 36 (top), 37, 38 (top), 41, 78 (right), 80 (top), 80 (bottom), 81 (bottom).

José António Rodrigues:
- pages: 9, 10, 25 (right), 31 (top), 32 (centre), 32 (bottom), 38 (bottom), 40 (top), 42, 44 (right), 45, 50 (top), 50 (bottom), 51(top), 64, 66 (left), 68, 69 (top), 75, 87 (bottom).

Nuno Sá:
- cover, pages: 6, 8 (left), 8 (bottom), 11, 13, 14, 16 (bottom), 17 (top), 18 (right), 19, 21, 25 (left), 26 (bottom), 30, 31 (bottom), 32 (top), 33, 34 (top), 35 (left), 36 (bottom), 39, 40 (bottom), 44 (left), 46, 47, 48, 49, 50 (centre), 51 (bottom), 52, 54, 55, 56, 57, 58, 60, 61, 62, 63, 66 (right), 67, 69 (bottom), 70, 72, 73, 74, 76, 78 (left), 79, 80 (centre), 81 (top), 82, 84, 85, 86, 87 (top).

With this book, Ver Açor continues to unveil the vast Azorean heritage, namely in terms of culture, religion, architecture and landscape. To all those who have helped us achieve our goal goes our deepest gratitude.